CHIP LOVITT

CREATIVE ☙ EDUCATION

Published by Creative Education
123 South Broad Street, Mankato, Minnesota 56001
Creative Education is an imprint of The Creative Company

Designed by Rita Marshall
Cover illustration by Rob Day

Photos by: Allsport Photography, Associated Press, Bettmann Archive,
Diane Johnson, Focus on Sports, Fotosport, and SportsChrome.

Library of Congress Cataloging-in-Publication Data

Lovitt, Chip.
Detroit Lions / by Chip Lovitt.
p. cm. — (NFL Today)
Summary: Traces the history of the team from its beginnings through 1996.
ISBN 0-88682-794-9

1. Detroit Lions (Football team)—History—Juvenile literature.
[1. Detroit Lions (Football team) 2. Football—History.]
I. Title. II. Series.

GV956.D4L68 1996   96-15235
796.332'64'0977434—dc20

123456

They call Detroit "the Motor City" because it is the car capital of the world. If it's an American car, it's a good bet that it was built in Detroit, home of the Big Three auto makers—Ford, General Motors and Chrysler. Cars are very important to Detroit's economy and to the economy of the entire state of Michigan.

But Detroit is more than just an automotive center. It is also a major international port. Goods are shipped from Detroit through the Great Lakes and up the St. Lawrence Seaway. In short, Detroit is a major commercial hub of the midwestern United States.

An all-time Lion great, Doak Walker.

Harry Ebding was the club's leading receiver during their inaugural season with 257 yards.

Detroit is also home to a football franchise that has been a symbol of strength in the National Football League (NFL) since the team was founded over sixty years ago. From the beginning, the Lions have left their mark on football history.

In 1934, George A. Richards, a Detroit radio tycoon and football enthusiast, bought the financially-ailing Portsmouth Spartans pro team and moved it to Detroit. Renamed the Lions, the team joined the NFL and got off to a roaring start in their very first season. They shut out their first seven opponents and won ten straight games. This exceptional performance placed them second only to the undefeated Chicago Bears.

The next season they finished first in the Western Division, then took on the powerful New York Giants for the league championship. As freezing rain turned the Detroit home field into a cold, muddy mess, the Lions mauled the Giants 26-7, winning their first NFL title.

The Lions' fortunes faded in the 1940s. But then, in 1950, the team acquired a new quarterback named Bobby Layne and a talented rookie running back, Doak Walker. The revamped Lions roster also included veteran end Leon Hart, a former Heisman Trophy winner, and a bruising two-way player who provided offensive and defensive muscle. Detroit was ready to dominate again.

LAYNE CHANGE

The team finished last in 1946, 1947 and 1948, and next to last in 1949. With Layne, Walker and Hart, the Lions climbed to a 6-6 record in 1950. Detroit hired Buddy Parker, who was a member of the Lions' 1935 championship team, as a new coach.

6   *Billy Sims was Rookie of the Year in 1980 (page 7).*

Parker knew how to motivate players. Under his leadership, the Lions finished second in 1951, just barely losing the Western Division title to the San Francisco 49ers, 21-17, on the final day of the season.

In 1952, Detroit fans expected the Lions to be contenders for the NFL championship, but early in the season the team lost twice to the 49ers and hardly looked like a winner. Then the Lions recovered, winning eight of their next nine games and claiming the Western Division title.

Ace Gutowsky led the Lions with 827 yards rushing.

The secret to their success was clear: Bobby Layne simply would not let them lose. Layne's career quarterbacking statistics may not match the all-time NFL leaders in touchdown passes or yardage, but the tough Texan was a born field general who could inspire his fellow players. He yelled at teammates, but he also joked with them. "I kid around a lot in the huddle because I don't like the pressure to build," Layne said. "I like to remind the guys of the good time we're gonna have when the games are over, things like that."

Layne loved to joke during practice, as well. One day Layne looked up and saw Les Bingaman, all 300 pounds of him, standing still during a drill. "Come on, Bing," Layne yelled. "Move around! You're killing the grass."

The Detroit quarterback never accepted defeat, never believed the Lions were going to lose. "Bobby never lost a game," remarked Doak Walker. "The clock just ran out on him a couple of times, that's all."

But the clock didn't run out on Layne and the Lions very often in 1952. They tied the Los Angeles Rams for first place in the Western Division. Then Layne led the Lions to a 31-21 playoff win over the Rams.

Detroit was set to battle the Cleveland Browns for the NFL championship. In the second quarter of that title game, Layne drove the Lions to the goal line, then plunged into the end zone on a quarterback sneak. The game was tied 7-7 when Doak Walker, who had been hurt much of the year, raced for a spectacular 67-yard touchdown. The Lions went on to win 17-7. In only his third season, Layne had led the Lions to their first NFL championship in 17 years.

1 9 5 0

Offensive sparkplug Doak Walker exploded for eleven touchdowns during the season.

The Lions won the Western Division title again in 1953, edging out Los Angeles. Again the Lions met the Cleveland Browns in the NFL title game. It was a game that would add glory to the Layne legend. With four minutes left in the game, Cleveland had a 16-10 lead. Layne trotted calmly onto the field and into the huddle. He looked at his teammates and saw fear in their eyes—fear of losing. That was something Bobby Layne never had.

Sensing that he needed to break the tension, Layne delivered a short, confident speech: "Now if you'll just block a little bit, fellas, ol' Bobby'll pass you right to the championship."

Layne did just that. In eight plays, he drove the Lions downfield, connecting with Jim Doran on a 33-yard TD pass to tie the game. Doak Walker kicked the extra point, and Detroit was the NFL champion for the second straight year.

Layne and the Lions won two more Western Division championships in 1954 and 1957. The 1954 team lost to Cleveland in the league championship game. The 1957 team brought Detroit its third NFL title of the 1950s, but it had to do so without Bobby Layne, who was injured during the season and replaced by Tobin Rote. Rote led Detroit to a 59-14 rout over Cleveland in the championship clash. After that, Layne never regained his place as

Barry Sanders was the greatest runner in Lions history (pages 10-11).

the Lions' star. He was traded in 1958, but remains Detroit's all-time leader in touchdown passes for a career (118).

Defensive tackle Alex Karras made his first Pro Bowl appearance.

KARRAS KILLS OFFENSES

Detroit struggled briefly after Layne's departure, but by 1960 the Lions were once again a winning team. They finished second in the Western Division in 1960, 1961 and 1962, and the team's new star was a defensive tackle named Alex Karras.

Karras was as strong as an ox and as blind as a bat. He wore thick glasses, but he left them off when he played. Even without his glasses, he never seemed to have any trouble locating running backs and quarterbacks and making their lives miserable.

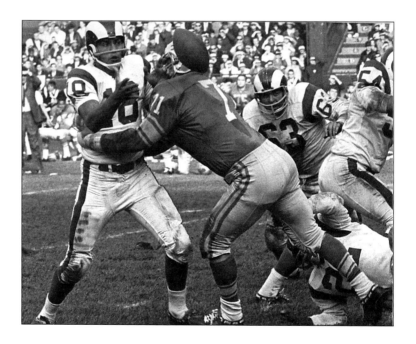

An All-Pro defender, Karras used his huge legs and tremendous strength to destroy offenses. Even though he weighed 270 pounds, Karras was incredibly fast. Offensive linemen could not match his speed. Sometimes, running backs couldn't either. "Running away from Karras is worse than running at him," said fleet-footed running back Lenny Moore of the Baltimore Colts. "He moves so fast on those stumpy legs, and you can hear him closing in on you from behind. I hate that sound. You get this feeling like you're about to be buried by a buffalo stampede."

After his fourth year in the Lions' starting lineup, defensive end Sam Williams left the club.

Karras was so good that he didn't often worry about the player trying to block him. He was only concerned with the quarterback, especially on pass plays. "If it's fairly sure to be a pass play," Karras said, "the quarterback's the one I'm thinking about. He's the guy I've got to get to. I can't think about the man in front of me. I've got to get around him as quickly as I can."

Karras, though, wasn't the only Lions defenseman with a reputation for being brutal and relentless. As nasty as Karras seemed, he wasn't as mean as linebacker Joe Schmidt. Schmidt was called "Red Dog" by sportswriters because of the way he tore into the enemy backfield.

Led by Schmidt and Karras, and assisted by talented players such as linebacker Wayne Walker, tackle Roger Brown and defensive backs Dick "Night Train" Lane and Yale Lary, the Detroit defense emerged as one of the toughest in the NFL.

On Thanksgiving Day in 1962, the Lions had a perfect opportunity to show how tough they were. Detroit was playing the Green Bay Packers, who had won their first ten games of the season. Still, the Lions were confident. "We'll beat the Packers," Schmidt said. "I know they've won ten games this season, but those ten games have nothing to do with game eleven." He was right.

In his rookie season, Billy Sims shredded opposing defenses for 1,303 rushing yards.

Leading 14-0, the Lions kept the pressure on Packers quarterback Bart Starr. In the second quarter, Karras and defensive ends Darris McCord and Sam Williams all hit Starr at once, forcing a fumble. Williams grabbed the ball and ran with it for a Lions touchdown. On Green Bay's next series, the Lions defense sacked Starr in the end zone for a safety. At halftime, Detroit sent the undefeated Packers into the locker rooms trailing 23-0. Detroit went on to win 26-14 in what one sportswriter called "one of the most memorable displays of aggressive defensive football ever witnessed."

Unfortunately, the Lions' stellar defense wasn't enough to carry the team to a division title. After winning the NFL championship in 1957, the Lions finished second in their division 11 times in the next 22 seasons. Although they boasted a top-notch team, the Lions couldn't find what they needed to make it back to first place.

SIMS BRINGS EXCITEMENT BACK TO DETROIT

The Lions started the 1970s with high hopes that they could put an end to their second-place frustrations. But as the decade progressed, the Lions found it increasingly difficult even to finish second. Many seasons, Detroit wound up losing as many games as it won. The Lions needed a new star to lead them back to the top.

In 1979, the Lions posted a 2-14 record, their worst ever. That was the bad news. The good news was that the Lions had the first pick in the 1980 NFL Draft. They selected a running back from the University of Oklahoma named Billy Sims. When he was a junior, Sims won the Heisman Trophy as the best college football player in the nation.

Linebacker Pat Swilling possessed exceptional speed and agility.

*Eddie Murray set a
team record with a
54-yard field goal.*

But Sims still had to prove himself as a pro. Early in his first regular season game, he did just that. After catching a short pass, Sims made a brilliant move to elude a linebacker, then raced for a 60-yard touchdown against the Los Angeles Rams defense. Detroit went on to win the game 41-20, and Detroit had found its new star.

The following week against Green Bay, Sims shined again as the Lions won 29-7. The Lions' record was 2-0. The previous year, without Sims, the Lions had won just two games all season. "I must admit," said coach Monte Clark, "as much as I like to stress team effort, Billy has been the big difference."

The Lions finished with a 9-7 record in 1980. Sims, who was named Rookie of the Year, scored 13 touchdowns and set a Lions rushing record with 1,303 yards.

In 1982, Sims led the Lions to their first playoff appearance since 1970. But in the first-round game, the Washington Redskins held Sims to just 19 yards and the Lions lost 31-7. The next season the Lions put it all together, winning their first division title since 1957.

In the playoffs, they met the San Francisco 49ers. Sims scored two touchdowns, and with just two minutes left, Detroit led 23-17. San Francisco quarterback Joe Montana responded by leading a touchdown march that put the 49ers back on top 24-23. But the Lions weren't finished yet. Quarterback Gary Danielson drove the Lions into field goal position with just five seconds left. The Lions then called on ace kicker Eddie Murray for the game-winning field goal. But Murray's kick missed by inches and the Lions' finest season in 25 years came to an end.

The following year, the Lions had a lot of luck—all bad. They lost several close games, and they lost Sims to a severe knee injury. He returned the following season, but the speed and

16

Placekicker Eddie Murray was the scoring leader throughout the 1980s.   17

spark in his running game were gone. Billy's career went down-hill and the Lions went down with him.

Detroit suffered through four more miserable seasons. Then, in 1989, the Lions found a new star. Like Billy Sims, he was a running back who wore number 20 on his jersey. Like Sims, he was fast, very fast. And like Sims, he didn't act like a big star. But make no mistake about it—as soon as Barry Sanders stepped into the spotlight, there was no doubt that he was destined to become one of the greatest running backs in the NFL.

SANDERS IS BARRY, BARRY GOOD

Until 1988, hardly anyone outside of Oklahoma State University had heard of Barry Sanders. That season, he gained an NCAA record 2,628 yards and scored an amazing

20

39 touchdowns. His performance earned him the Heisman Trophy.

Detroit had the number two draft pick in 1988 and used it to grab Sanders. Despite his relatively small size, Sanders proved to be both powerful and fast. He was also incredibly agile, which enabled him to elude many would-be tacklers. Sanders made a great first impression on many NFL veterans.

"He reminds me of a guy we used to have," said Chicago Bears coach Mike Ditka, comparing Barry to Walter Payton, the NFL's all-time leading rusher. "He's better than I was," Payton replied. "I was never that good."

Sanders kept getting better, and so did the Lions. They won six of their last seven games in 1989, and in the last game of the season, Sanders broke Billy Sims' Lions rookie rushing record. The contest was stopped and a familiar figure came onto the field to present Sanders with the game ball. It was Billy Sims.

"He's the greatest," Sims said of Sanders. "No," Sanders said as he shook Sims' hand, "you're the greatest."

Sanders finished his debut season with 1,470 yards rushing, second-best in the NFL. It was no surprise when he was named Rookie of the Year.

Sanders wasted no time showing the world that his first season was no fluke. In his first six years, Barry Sanders rushed for 8,672 yards, an average of 1,445 yards per season. Even in 1993, when he injured his knee and missed five games, he still racked up 1,115 yards. And in 1994, Sanders rushed for 1,883 yards, the fourth-best total in NFL history. He was a Pro Bowl selection in each of his first six seasons.

With Sanders powering the Lions, the team finished 12-4 to win the NFC Central Division title in 1991. Not only was it the

1 9 8 9

Chris Spielman led the club in tackles for the second straight season.

Tackle Lomas Brown was a longtime Lions star.

team's first winning season since 1983, it was also Detroit's best finish ever. In 1993, the Lions won the NFC Central Division title again but were knocked out of the playoffs by the Packers.

Sanders has a big fan club among NFL coaches and players. "Barry Sanders is one of a kind," said his coach, Wayne Fontes. "I've seen them all. I watch miles and miles of film. I see hundreds each year. He's the best I've ever seen."

Super-athlete Bo Jackson agreed. "When I grow up, I want to be just like him," Jackson said. "Barry's my new idol; I like the way he runs. He's a water bug out there the way he moves."

If Sanders keeps piling up rushing yards at his current pace, he's a sure shot for the Pro Football Hall of Fame. If he's selected, he'll join three other Lions—defensive backs Lem Barney and Jack Christiansen and quarterback and former Lion coach, Earl "Dutch" Clark.

Lions defensive back Bennie Blades made 95 tackles and grabbed three interceptions.

FOCUS: THE SUPPORTING CAST

While Sanders was the big star, Detroit knew they had to strengthen the overall team for him to be successful. They continued to rebuild their roster in the 1990s, blending a mix of seasoned veterans and younger players. On defense, linebackers Chris Spielman, Pat Swilling and Tracy Scroggins developed into feared pass rushers, and hard-hitting safety Bennie Blades added depth in the secondary. Offensive tackle Lomas Brown, a three-time All-Pro, opened up holes for Barry Sanders. Wide receiver Brett Perriman combined speed with precision moves, while Herman Moore—a star high jumper in college— used his leaping ability to make spectacular catches.

In the early 1990s, the Lions rotated several players at quarterback, but none of them were able to nail down the starting

Left to right: Chris Spielman, Brett Perriman, Barry Sanders, Jimmy Williams.

spot. Prior to the 1994 season, the Lions signed quarterback Scott Mitchell to an $11 million contract and coach Wayne Fontes named him as the starter. Mitchell, who had been the Miami Dolphins' backup quarterback behind Dan Marino, had long wanted to emerge from Marino's shadow. The Lions offered him the chance.

"From the time I was a little kid," Mitchell said upon his arrival in Detroit, "I've always dreamed of being a starting quarterback in the NFL. I came to Detroit to win. I came to be here with people who can win."

"We're very fortunate to get this young man," Wayne Fontes said. "This guy is hopefully the missing piece of the puzzle that one day will put the Lions into the Super Bowl."

The Lions' 1994 season was indeed a puzzle. At the beginning of December, the team was 5-6 and Mitchell was struggling. His 48.4 percent passing completion rate put him dead last in the NFL. Veteran Dave Krieg stepped in as the backup quarterback and the team focused on a late-season run for the playoffs.

The 1995 season got off to a dismal start, with the Lions losing their first three games and stumbling to a 3-6 mark with only seven games left in the season. A losing record seemed certain. Both quarterback Scott Mitchell and coach Wayne Fontes came under fire from fans and the media. Team owner William Clay Ford issued an ultimatum: Make the playoffs, or there would be big changes, starting with coach Wayne Fontes.

A turning point came in November. Riding a two-game winning streak, the Lions took on the Minnesota Vikings. Scott Mitchell launched an all-out 410-yard, four touchdown pass air assault, hitting receivers Brett Perriman, Herman Moore and

1 9 9 4

Wide receiver Brett Perriman caught 56 passes and emerged as an NFL star.

Brett Perriman is one of the Lions' best openfield runners (page 26-27).

Jason Hanson led the Lions in scoring with 93 points.

Johnnie Morton for more than 100 yards apiece. Barry Sanders, held to just one yard in the first half, rushed for 138 yards, including a 50-yard touchdown romp. The Vikings scored early and often, but the Lions' sustained effort gave them a 44-38 victory.

Mitchell's 410 passing yards topped Bobby Layne's 35-year-old team record of 375. But what made Mitchell's performance even more impressive was the fact that he was playing on an injured ankle. "Anyone who doesn't think Scott Mitchell is tough enough is welcome to put on my uniform and try him out," Moore stated. "Scott's taken a lot of heat this year, but I think he proved what a competitor he is."

Mitchell and Moore kept the Lions in the hunt for a playoff spot. The team won its final seven games, finishing 10-6 to earn second place in the Central Division—and a Wild Card play-off spot. During the regular season, Detroit's league-leading offense had amassed an amazing 6,113 yards. Moore led the NFL in receiving and set an NFL record with 123 catches. His 1,686 receiving yards (a team record), combined with Brett Perriman's 1,488, were the most ever by a pair of NFL team-mates. Barry Sanders, as usual, had an excellent season, gaining 1,500 yards, second only to Emmitt Smith. Scott Mitchell, with 32 touchdown passes, broke Bobby Layne's old team mark of 26.

The Lions made the playoffs, but their Super Bowl dreams were short-lived. In the first round, the Philadelphia Eagles mauled the Lions. Down 51-7 in the third quarter, the Lions battled back but lost 58-37. (The combined 95-point total was the most ever in an NFL playoff game.)

Making it to the playoffs was a solid achievement, but it was not the ultimate goal, as Barry Sanders attested.

Herman Moore was a record breaking receiver.   29

Henry Thomas was a pass rushing specialist.

The premier running back in the NFL, Barry Sanders.

1 9 9 7

Running back Glyn Milburn brings his speed and versatility from the Broncos.

"History has shown that a lot of great players have played the game, but a lot fewer of those guys had a chance to play in the Super Bowl," Sanders said. "So when you really get down to it, that's what drives most of the people around the league. It's an empty feeling to sit home and watch."

The Lions players and coaches have no intention of sitting home to watch the Super Bowl. Their plan is to be there playing. So far, that goal has eluded the Lions. But Detroit is a hard-nosed, blue-collar city that has battled adversity throughout its history and continued to come out on top. With their football sights set on the Super Bowl, neither the Lions nor their loyal Motor City fans will be satisfied with anything less.